Why PRAISE HIM (GOD)

Purpose of Praise

PASTOR JOYCE WALLER

ISBN 979-8-88943-283-8 (paperback)
ISBN 979-8-88943-284-5 (digital)

Christian Faith Publishing
832 Park Avenue
Meadville, PA 16335
www.christianfaithpublishing.com

The scriptures are from Bible Gateway, https://www.biblegateway.com/passage/?search=Habakkuk+3&version=KJV.

Printed in the United States of America

In loving memory of
Grandparents Rufus and Mamie Waller
Two brothers Steve and Marvin Waller
Devoted church member Julia Sanford
Father Durell Ingram

Abstract

Each of us has experienced difficult times in our lives. Life is full of unexpected interruptions that can be confusing, challenging, and mind-boggling, which can lead us to the make wrong discission.

Preface

The Lord has inspired me to write this book for His glory. Many are often wondering, Why praise Him (God)? Praise is something that is learned through many trials and many errors and many pitfalls in a person's life. We sing with choir, and we love our praise dancer. One known fact: the old spiritual hymns are filed with true praises of God.

Old spiritual hymns give order in church the same way when any leader of service enters a room. So why praise Him (God)? Well, until you know the story, only then will you understand why praise Him (God).

This book is dedicated to my loving family: Daisy, Antraun, Andrea, Eleisha, and Shamar; and also my loving church family who have been there with me through the storm. Thank you all.

Chapter 1

God Sees Me

I know the Lord is watching over me and will continue watching over me until He brings me home to His kingdom. This is one of my encounters with God and how I began to realize every situation has a significant purpose. I know He saw me before I became saved.

I had asked my cousin if he would put brakes on my car, and he said, "Sure, bring your car over to my mom's house." So when I arrived there, he wasn't there. I waited for him, and finally he showed up and stated he couldn't do it. Mind you, I had waited until my brakes were scrubbings with a loud noise. I know in my mind if I drove this car to a shop, I wasn't going to make it. I did what any person would do: I prayed, "Lord, help me get my car to the shop." I was very nervous about moving my car, but I got into the car, closed door, put on my seat belt, put the key into the ignition, and turned the key. The car was running well. Then I pulled the gear handle in reverse and started backing up out of the driveway; and when I put my car in drive, out of the blue, I heard a strange sound. My foot was no longer pushing the brakes; my car was driving me.

My car jumped up and was speeding down the driveway. I was in a panic, no brakes, and I could not control the steering wheel that day. I missed a gas tank, did not go into my aunt's garage, swiped the sidesteps alongside her house. My car veered to the right and was speeding out of control across her yard. At that moment, I knew I was about to be killed in my car. Suddenly out of nowhere, I felt something snatch my car backward, pulling the car back until it stopped. I couldn't do anything but sit in my car and look toward heaven and say, "Thank you," with tears flooding down my cheeks. I was scared out of my mind.

When my life finally came back into my body, I got out of my car and looked to see what had grabbed my car that day. The fear was unbelievable, and while I was walking around my car, my feet were shaking like leaves on a tree. I could not find any evidence of what had grabbed my car. There wasn't anything attached under my car, and nothing was wrapped around my tires. This incident still has my mind puzzled to the present. I was very grateful and appreciative that the Lord spared my life for a little while longer. Also, He allowed me a little more time with my family. Because He spared my life, I was able to attend my children's and grandson's graduation. This milestone was made possible by my Lord. There were some rough patches along the way, much failure, much disappointment, friends lost, loved ones passed on to glory, but through it all, He gets the glory and praise.

I did not know the plans that God had for my life. At the moment, I was going to get know Him in such a significant way that I was going to be so amazed. I just didn't know when it was going to take place or what I had do for him. I pondered all night long about what had just happened with my car and still could not arrive at a conclusion. God saw something in me that I had no idea existed. He chose me for a journey that would give Him glory in more ways than one. I recognize now that "Thank You, Lord" is not enough; we must give Him praise for every outcome that we encounter, whether good or bad. Praise Him while you have a chance.

Chapter 2

God Sees Me

> After these things the word of the LORD came unto Abram in a vision, saying, Fear not, Abram: I am thy shield, and thy exceeding great reward.
>
> And Abram said, LORD God, what wilt thou give me, seeing I go childless, and the steward of my house is this Eliezer of Damascus?
>
> And Abram said, Behold, to me thou hast given no seed: and, lo, one born in my house is mine heir.
>
> And, behold, the word of the LORD came unto him, saying, This shall not be thine heir; but he that shall come forth out of thine own bowels shall be thine heir. (Genesis 15:1–4 KJV)

He believed what God spoke about his seed, and it was counted as righteousness toward him. Abraham had to share with Sarah the plans that God spoke with him about having a seed. When a person receives a vision from God, the vision has a way of taking root, and it brings forth excitement and joy and great expectation in a person's life. A person who designs any infrastructure is given a vision, and that vision then translated into pencil on paper or in technology. Then the vision becomes a glorious tall building with a unique structure. The world adores it. Sarah was excited about conceiving a child with her husband and then saw herself not worthy of caring for a child. Sarah physically talked herself out of the vision all because she noticed obstacles in her way like her age and her body. Oftentimes we forget who gave the vision in the first place.

Also, she had to have a conversation with herself before allowing Hagar to become her husband's wife. Sarah had to ponder on this situation for a while before she gave her consent. Sarah chose Hagar to be her husband's wife so he could have a child. Sarah saw an innocent situation, but when reality set in, it became a blindside for both women.

> And she called the name of the LORD that spake unto her, Thou God seest me: for she said, Have I also here looked after him that seeth me? (Genesis 16:13 KJV)

Hagar was a very unique woman and had a small role in the Bible, but what God did for her is so amazing. Hagar found herself in a difficult situation that she did not ask for: Sarah became very jealous of Hagar when she noticed that Hagar had conceived a child with Abraham. Sarah went to her husband and "said unto Abram, My wrong be upon thee: I have given my maid into thy bosom" (Genesis 16:5).

Sarai made Hagar's life so miserable to the point where she had to leave their presence. I believe every time Hagar did something, Sarah complained about it and made Hagar's life a living nightmare until she walked out one day. One thing I can say about the Lord: He will take care of His people every single time. While Hagar was walking and thinking about why she left her home, the Spirit of Lord met her. Be assured He will do the same thing for you; it doesn't matter where your previous life's story begins. God loves you. Hagar did not even know why Sarah was acting the way she was acting. Clearly, she was not aware of the true reason why Sarah allowed her to marry her husband, and she did not know she was carrying Abraham's child.

Hagar met God, and the Spirit of the Lord asked her two questions: "Where did you come from?" Hagar stated, "I flee from the face of my mistress Sarai" (Genesis 16:8). But when the Spirit of the Lord asked her where she will go, Hagar did not have an answer.

The Word informs us that He will never leave us, and that is true. The Spirit informed Hagar that she was with child and gave a name for the child. He spoke blessing upon her child and also informed her to return and submit to Sarah. God told Hagar, "I will multiply thy seed exceedingly, that it shall not be numbered for multitude." All because Hagar was carrying Abraham's seed, this put her and her child in line for a blessing. So Hagar returned and submitted to Sarah. Remember, God does the multiplying in a person's life.

> According as he hath chosen us in him before the
> foundation of the world, that we should be holy
> and without blame before him in love: Having
> predestinated us unto the adoption of children
> by Jesus Christ to himself, according to the good
> pleasure of his will. (Ephesian 1:4–5)

The Lord has chosen us to be His people, but it is your decision to serve Him. God is not going to make anyone serve Him; that has to be of *your own free will.*

Bring the vision to life. Hagar had a son named Ishmael, and blessings followed him just as the word spoken to her. Ishmael grew up, and the Ishmaelites were named after him.

Chapter 3

Joyful Noise

O come, let us sing unto the Lord: let us make a joyful noise to the rock of our salvation. Let us come before his presence with thanks giving and make a joyful noise unto him with psalms. (Psalm 95:1–2 KJV)

Every church has one single person who would set the church on fire when he or she begins to sing. It only takes one person to stand up and start rocking with the beat, and there would be two plus four plus twelve—and most of the church will be well into praising God and others just there! We need music because we were brought up on it. There's nothing like singing and dancing to music. Whether R&B, gospel, rock, country, or whatever genre you like, music will make you move every single time. It does not matter how old you are, music will make the body rock. We exist because of a *Sound*. God said, "Let it be." We listen to music when we are sad or happy or just for the fun of it.

As we learn to praise God, we know He is worthy to be praised. Therefore, hearing the right kind gospel music well move upon our hearts regardless of our emotions.

I believe I created a waterfall in my vehicle many of days. I was listening to radio, and Bishop Paul Morton's song "Be Blessed" came on out of the blue. As I was listening to the words *encourage* and *depend,* I became relaxed and started praising God and remembering

His words that He has over my life: "I will never leave you nor forsake you." Also I was remembering the many blessings that the Lord had delivered into my life.

Omnipresence describes God being present in our everyday life.

Chapter 4

Accepting the Call

Here is a man who was against the church and did not mind letting the people know, and his name was Saul. Saul brought destruction with him, and Christians were afraid of him. They had to learn the Word of God in secret. This one man had one purpose: persecute the church. He walked and talked with the authority that was given to him by man and had the ability to carry it out and was not afraid to enter into people's homes looking for anyone who had faith in God and would haul them to jail. Wow, the power he demonstrated was so remarkable, and we wonder why Jesus would save a man like this. It is for the *same* reason He wants to save you.

> And when we were all fallen to the earth, I heard a voice speaking unto me, and saying in the Hebrew tongue, Saul, Saul, why persecutest thou me? it is hard for thee to kick against the pricks. And I said, Who art thou, Lord? And he said, I am Jesus whom thou persecutest. (Acts 9:14–15 KJV)

Saul did not have a clue what was going to change in his life. It is so devastating that we have to be brought down low in order to look up the to the hills. Just keep living, and you may find a reason to praise Him and discover it is all worth it. Stop for a moment and let us pray: "Lord, help us to realize there is a better way of living and give us knowledge and wisdom to understand how to make that change, in Jesus's name, amen."

After reading this text, I realize God will send His Son to intervene Satan's plan for harm over our life. If we would keep the faith, God will deliver us every single time. Saul heard Jesus.

When was the first time you heard the Lord's voice? The first time when I heard God's voice, I was at Piggly Wiggly grocery store walking down the aisle with my buggy, minding my own business. Just out of the blue, I heard this distinct voice communicating with me. I thought to myself, *Am I losing it?* The shocker: the Lord was reminding me of all my wrongdoing, but I was putting different items in a buggy. It appears as if I was in a trance among the people.

I arrived at the cashier and checkout and paid little of nothing for all those groceries that I had. Here is the punchline that the Lord informed me that day. He stated, *I want you to go to club tonight, and don't drink anything because I want to show you something*. Yes, it was a Saturday, so I did just that. You know what? Around 1:00 a.m., while I was standing against a wall wanting to shake my groove thing, the DJ played my jam. Then suddenly, I heard the Lord say, *Look around you. Look at this woman and that woman, how they are partying, drinking, and dancing*. I did just that, and He said, *This is what you look like when you party, drink, and dance*. Wow, I was so shocked because the women's facial appearance was droopy, their makeup smeared, eyelashes hanging off their eyelids. Also, the women's gait was very unsteady, and no one was minding their surroundings. About five minutes later, two women started arguing over some man, and it was time for me leave. Remember, sin stinks regardless of who's carrying it.

Jesus asks a powerful question: "Why persecutest me?" What we do not realize is, Jesus is the church. The building is a place for accommodation for the saints to assemble together to worship God. Regardless of how you feel about a church, it will not stop God from blessing His people and using you to help bless them. Any past hurt you may be experiencing is nothing at all. It is in the past, and guess what? Please leave it alone. You cannot undo any past faults, but we have a Redeemer, and His name is Jesus. He died for you to have the right to walk into His Father's kingdom just as one of the thieves on the cross with Him. He defended Jesus that day on the cross, and just like that, he earned a front-row pass into heaven.

It is strange for Saul to ask, "Who art thou, Lord?" and then answer his own question. Jesus told him it is hard to kick against the pricks (it is hard trying to stop people from learning or teaching the Word). Pharoah could not stop it, King Harold could not do it, and Satan definitely could not do it. So what does this tell you? The earth and the fullness thereof belongs to the Lord. There is no way you can stop God's Word from being illuminated.

Chapter 5

Being Equipped

> But rise, and stand upon thy feet: for I have appeared unto thee for this purpose, to make thee a minister and a witness both of these things which thou hast seen, and of those things in the which I will appear unto thee;
>
> Delivering thee from the people, and from the Gentiles, unto whom now I send thee,
>
> To open their eyes, and to turn them from darkness to light, and from the power of Satan unto God, that they may receive forgiveness of sins, and inheritance among them which are sanctified by faith that is in me. (Acts 9:16–18 KJV)

Jesus told Saul everything that he was going to accomplish: for instance, he would minister, witness, deliver, open eyes, receive forgiveness, and have inheritance. It is amazing how he accomplishes every single task that was assigned to him by the Lord. The pressure Paul was under wasn't easy, but he kept on preaching, kept on writing to the church, kept on praying, kept on walking, and kept on winning souls to Christ. Whatever the Lord has chosen for you to do, *believe* that you have what it takes. Saul became blind and did not eat for three days. God had a plan for his life that was so fascinating, but Saul had to have a willingness to change.

The change begins with you. Saul became Paul with a power anointing. There is one point everyone needs to know: there will always be a condition in your life that will lead you to depend on the Lord, which indicates you won't desire Him until something turns for the worst. When opportunities arrive beyond our control, this is where we all become frustrated and annoyed. It does not matter where you are spiritually; awful things have a way of entering our lives. Each of us will feel the pressure that leads to the Lord in a deep prayer for a powerful breakthrough. Only when you have tried everyone and everything else will you know that you need to pray, trust, believe, and have faith in the Lord.

Chapter 6

Prayer Changes Things

Then Ananias answered, Lord, I have heard by many of this man, how much evil he hath done to thy saints at Jerusalem: and here he hath authority from the chief priests to bind all that call on thy name.

But the Lord said unto him, Go thy way: for he is a chosen vessel unto me, to bear my name before the Gentiles, and kings, and the children of Israel: for I will shew him how great things he must suffer for my name's sake.

And Ananias went his way, and entered into the house; and putting his hands on him said, Brother Saul, the Lord, even Jesus, that appeared unto thee in the way as thou camest, hath sent me, that thou mightest receive thy sight, and be filled with the Holy Ghost. (Acts 9:13–17 KJV)

An anointed touch. Regardless of Ananias's feeling, God had already chosen Saul for a vessel for Him. God has chosen many of us for His purpose. God told Jerimiah:

"For I know the plans I have for you," declares the LORD, "plans to prosper you and not to

harm you, plans to give you hope and a future."
(Jeremiah 29:11 KJV)

Praise Him (God) for a change in the right direction in your life. This path that God offers is difficult to walk on, but you can handle it. Do not allow so-called friends to stop you from achieving a new life or a new version of yourself. After Ananias put his hand on Saul, the Holy Ghost came through Ananias and entered Saul, and Saul was transformed into Paul. That same fiery passion that Saul had in the past was now used for God's glory.

After Paul gained his strength, he started toward the church and entered it and started preaching the Word of Jesus. He had man's authority to enter people's homes and bind them for the Word, but he was given God's authority to enter homes and churches to win souls for Christ. His transformation is what made Paul a danger man. Paul's journey was so amazing that he wrote thirteen books in the Bible, and every step he made was in the right direction to God's people, teaching that Jesus died on cross for our sins and your life can be redeemed.

Chapter 7

Willingness to Change

I beseech you therefore, brethren, by the mercies of God, that ye present your bodies a living sacrifice, holy, acceptable unto God, which is your reasonable service.

And be not conformed to this world: but be ye transformed by the renewing of your mind, that ye may prove what is that *good*, and *acceptable, and perfect, will of God*. (Roman 12:1–2 KJV, emphasis added)

With a willingness to change, anyone who wants a new start in life can change. It takes a well-made-up mind to change for the right reason. Why praise Him? Praise Him (God) for a change in the right direction for your life. When you make this change, let it be for you and no one else. Often many people will attempt to change for other people instead for the one who really matters—yourself.

Why keep doing the same thing over and over again and reaching the same outcome? Why continue to do harmful things that do not profit anything? Paul is teaching us to change the way we think by "renewing your mind."

Your life is so important to the Father; that is why He gave us Jesus. The Lord wants what is best for you. He wants His people to be saved.

It is so easy to be caught in this lavish big world. This world has a lot to offer, but it is your decision, whether good or bad, how to go about it. It does not matter where you begin, but where and how you finish should be so amazing. Paul teaches us not to be conformed to this world but to be transformed by renewing our mind. Change the way you think. Praise Him for His glory and His grace and mercy over your life.

It may take you to march around your room seeking Him and asking Him to come into your life. You're not worthy because "we have all sinned and come short of His glory," but the love God has for you is so outstanding it will blow your mind. Thank You, Jesus!

It is hard to put down evil things because it feels so good to us. Sometimes it is hard to see why you need to change. It is so important for you to change the way you think by training your mind to think about positive things instead of negative things. The Word of God teaches us how to think:

> Whatsoever things are true, whatsoever things are honest, whatsoever things are just, whatsoever things are pure, whatsoever things are lovely, whatsoever things are of good report; if there be any virtue, and if there be any praise, think on these things. (Philippians 4:8 KJV)

This scripture is letting us know how valuable Jesus is to us. If we would only think about good times and laughter and joyous occasions, we shall overcome. Know that change is good and repeat—change is good and know change is good. Do not get caught up in wrongful thinking. Do not let the enemy play with your mind. And most importantly, you are a winner. Why praise Him? He is worthy of praise, and find faith in Him.

Chapter 8

Know God Is Your Supplier

I know it's difficult developing a relationship with God—especially when you have tried going to a church but heard disturbing news about it: there are members with funny attitudes, and people are not in-tuned to the Gospel as grandma used to be. But finding favor with God through His Son, Jesus, and accepting the Holy Spirit in your life will be the *best* decision you will ever make.

Let's take a journey and visit with a powerful man of God whose name is Elijah after he had spoken to King Ahab that "there shall not be rain or dew but according to my word." God deals with each of us differently, and each person has a unique character. God spoke to Elijah and told him to get to a river. God then stated, "I have commanded the raven to feed you there."

> And the word of the LORD came unto him, saying, Get thee hence, and turn thee eastward, and hide thyself by the brook Cherith, that is before Jordan. And it shall be, that thou shalt drink of the brook; and I have commanded the ravens to feed thee there.
>
> So he went and did according unto the word of the LORD: for he went and dwelt by the brook Cherith, that is before Jordan. And the ravens brought him bread and flesh in the morning, and

bread and flesh in the evening; and he drank of
the brook. (1 Kings 17:1–6 KJV)

Can you imagine the expression that Elijah must have had on
his face? If you noticed in this text, Elijah did not take any belongings with him. Therefore, his faith and trust in God was remarkable.
God gave a command, and Elijah followed His orders. There is not
one person who does not struggle with orders. We need orders to
survive regardless of how someone may feel about it.

Elijah did not take time to wonder how but stepped out in
faith. He knew God's word is bond. Church, when will we get there?
We need to move in the right direction to give praise to our Lord for
our everyday needs. I do not know how the raven supplied food for
him or where they got it from, but meat and bread appeared twice a
day until the river dried up. Then God told him to leave there and
that he had sustained a widow to continue to supply Elijah's needs.
The vast majority of us know what it is like to struggle and how hard
it was to overcome our disbeliefs. We have lost sight of our Creator,
but He is still sitting high and looking low. Most amazing—He never
stops blessing or healing or delivering His people regardless of how
we may treat Him.

But without faith it is impossible to please him:
for he that cometh to God must believe that he
is, and that he is a rewarder of them that dili-
gently seek him. (Hebrews 11:6 KJV)

Then he took the five loaves and the two fishes,
and looking up to heaven, he blessed them, and
brake, and gave to the disciples to set before the
multitude.

And they did eat, and were all filled: and
there was taken up of fragments that remained to
them twelve baskets. (Luke 9:16–17 KJV)

The disciples were concerned about feeding five thousand because of the quantity, but Jesus saw quality in five loaves and two fish. Why? Because He knows His Father would supply. First Jesus gave thanks, and then He blessed it and then issued out food, and everyone's belly was full.

In the midst of all that, there were twelve baskets of food left over. How did two fish and five loaves of bread feed five thousand? Jesus saw an opportunity for His Father to get the glory from this. Everything Jesus did was for His Father's glory. Why praise Him? Praise Him because He is our supplier. Take a moment to look around you—what is missing from your table? Give God praise and know He will supply your every need.

Lord, I don't know how You are going to supply my needs, but I will trust You to the best of my ability. But just in case I lose sight, please forgive me and have mercy on my soul, in Jesus's name, amen.

Chapter 9

Praise Him While You Have a Chance

Why praise Him? Learning to praise Him is so significant to everyone's life, whether we like it or not. Take a moment and think about it. You want to be praised for your great work or rewarded. You also enjoy a pat on the back or somebody saying "Well done." So why praise Him? *Because He is worthy.*

> Wherefore God also hath highly exalted him, and given him a name which is above every name: that at the name of Jesus every knee should bow, of things in heaven, and things in earth, and things under the earth; and that every tongue should confess that Jesus Christ is Lord, to the glory of God the Father.
>
> Wherefore, my beloved, as ye have always obeyed, not as in my presence only, but now much more in my absence, work out your own salvation with fear and trembling. (Philippians 2:9–12)

The truth is, whether we like it or not, the day shall come when we are all going to give praise to Him for who He is and for His achievements on the cross. We will bow before the Heavenly Father and praise Him. Countless people are going to be shouting, "Lord, I am sorry for not believing. Please forgive me and give me another chance!" But you know what? It is time to get to know the Lord for yourself and make up your own mind. The Word informs us in Malachi 3:10:

> Bring ye all the tithes into the storehouse, that there may be meat in mine house, and prove me now herewith, saith the LORD of hosts, if I will not open you the windows of heaven, and pour you out a blessing, that there shall not be room enough to receive it.

God has a way of bringing his words to life in everyone's life. Why praise Him?

> For great is the LORD and most worthy of praise;
> he is to be feared above all gods.
> For all the gods of the nations are idols,
> but the LORD made the heavens. (1 Chronicles 16:25–26 KJV)

> Weeping may endure for a night, but joy cometh
> in the morning. (Psalm 30:5 KJV)

I know it is so hard to witness a breakthrough, especially when you are in the storm. Learn to praise your way out. Stop for a moment. Lord, I want to praise You and sing praises to Your name, but I do not know how, so teach me. Always listen for that still but powerful voice. I have learned that the Lord always, without a shadow of a doubt, will speak to your heart. Once you have this experience, you will feel the increasing love that He has toward you.

Chapter 10

God Who Delivers— Shadrach, Meshach, and Abednego Taking a Stand

Then these men were bound in their coats, their hosen, and their hats, and their other garments, and were cast into the midst of the burning fiery furnace.

Therefore because the king's commandment was urgent, and the furnace exceeding hot, the flames of the fire slew those men that took up Shadrach, Meshach, and Abednego.

And these three men, Shadrach, Meshach, and Abednego, *fell down bound into the midst of the burning fiery furnace*. (Daniel 3:21–23 KJV, emphasis added)

I know this a lot of information, but reading this particular text may help you understand that He will deliver you. We must know these are three young men who have been taught by their parents to serve God and Him only. They never wavered, which means they trusted the Lord without a shadow of a doubt. When they heard about the king's decree that after sounding all kinds of music, everyone must fall down and worship the golden image, it is amazing that their mind was already made up not to worship the golden image but to worship the Lord only. They held on to what they knew about the Lord. They paid no mind to the consequences but kept their faith in the Lord. Most of all, these young men were already working for the king and were fully aware of the consequence. It was no surprise to them, but they did what we dream about doing—holding on to faith and not letting fear overtake us.

The question is, How does one put trust in the Lord? One must believe. One must have faith to know God is the true God, and He gave us Jesus and the Holy Spirit. We should be able to confess openly that Jesus is the Son of God

How does one develop this trust? It is significant that one must be taught the Word of God. One must read, attend church, attend Sunday school, and attend Bible study. The book of James informs us that faith without works is dead.

These three men were already in high positions in the king kingdom and were fully aware of the king's decree and of the punishment, but they did not hide who they were. They chose *not* to fall down and worship the golden image and were, because of this, brought before the king.

What are you going to do about your situation?

These three young men were brought before king in all their belongings by the three strongest men the king had. Their hands were tied behind their backs—all because they refused to bow down and worship the golden image. Remember, the furnace was heated up seven times hotter than usual. Now, in our mind, a furnace may be what we have seen over years resembling an old furnace, with a door where wood is placed. However, text furnace is a big open area below a hill. The king was able to look down into this furnace.

When the three soldiers brought the three Hebrew boys up the top hill overlooking the furnace, the flames were so high. The heat from the flames automatically consumed the three soldiers, but God's grace covered the Hebrew boys. This did not stop them from falling into the furnace because when the soldiers lost grip, they lost grip; but once again God's grace sustained them. Anybody who is willing to give his life for Lord is so worthy of God's protection. God told Jesus to provide protection over those Hebrew boys every step of the way.

The king's words were, "Who is this God who will deliver you out of my hand?" He is Alpha and Omega, the First and Last, the Beginning and the End.

He is in the room right now with you. Get up and praise Him. Wave your hands and open up your mouth because He is worthy!

God's grace sustains the Hebrew boys while they were falling into fire. I can only imagine the look on their faces when they realized they were still living as they fell into furnace. The greater perspective is, when they arrived at the bottom of the pit, the fire continued to burn around them, and still they were living. You know, one of them asked a question, "Man, are we dead and now a spirit? How is this possible?" I believe they began to touch one another, and their minds were blown beyond comprehension. In a second, those boys recognized that the Lord is worthy to be praised.

Those boys, along with Jesus, got up and shook the dust off and started dancing and praising God loudly. Did you notice not once did God stop them from falling but instead provided a cushion for them? Church, there are times when you must go through a trial and learn to give Him glory.

I know it is hard to praise God in a difficult and impossible circumstance. Child, yes, it is, but He still remains the same and receives glory every single time because He is worthy to be praised.

I believe it was the sound of praising that grabbed the king's ears, and while he was easing up out of his seat, he kept listening to the praising and started moving toward that magnificent sound. My God, when he came to the mouth of the fiery furnace, he looked at God's grace protecting king, nobody but God.

The king was astonished at the fourth man looking like the Son of God. Baby, He is the Son of God marching with his servants, giving God all the praise and all the glory. Church, did you notice the fire never went out? And neither did God's grace ever leave them.

Church, it may be hard, but you will survive. Most of all, *patience is a virtue.*

Chapter 11

Then Nebuchadnezzar the king was astonished, and rose up in haste, and spake, and said unto his counsellors, Did not we cast three men bound into the midst of the fire? They answered and said unto the king, True, O king.

He answered and said, Lo, I see four men loose, walking in the midst of the fire, and they have no hurt; and the form of the fourth is like the Son of God.

Then Nebuchadnezzar came near to the mouth of the burning fiery furnace, and spake, and said, Shadrach, Meshach, and Abednego, ye servants of the most high God, come forth, and come hither. Then Shadrach, Meshach, and Abednego, came forth of the midst of the fire.

And the princes, governors, and captains, and the king's counsellors, being gathered together, saw these men, upon whose bodies the fire had no power, nor was an hair of their head singed, neither were their coats changed, nor the smell of fire had passed on them.

Then Nebuchadnezzar spake, and said, Blessed be the God of Shadrach, Meshach, and Abednego, who hath sent his angel, and delivered his servants that trusted in him, and have changed the king's word, and yielded their bodies, that they might not serve nor worship any god, except their own God.

Therefore I make a decree, That every people, nation, and language, which speak any thing amiss against the God of Shadrach, Meshach, and Abednego, shall be cut in pieces, and their houses shall be made a dunghill: because there is no other God that can deliver after this sort.

Then the king promoted Shadrach, Meshach, and Abednego, in the province of Babylon. (Daniel 3:24–30 KJV)

In verse 26, the king called for the three Hebrew boys to come forth out of the fiery furnace, and did you read where the flames were put out? What God demonstrated to us here is that through it all, He will not leave you at any time. Those Hebrew boys fell in the fire, but they walked out of fire with victory. Wow, Jesus showed up as Spirit, and He has power beyond anyone's imagination. His presence is what sustained them in the fire. These young men held on to their faith, and God blessed them accordingly. Therefore, continue to praise the Lord regardless of people's opinion. Keep in mind, everyone has a choice to make whether to serve the Lord or not.

And he answered and said unto them, I tell you that, if these should hold their peace, the stones would immediately cry out. (Luke 19:40 KJV)

Somebody somewhere will always be giving God glory. Why? Because He is worthy to be praised. You cannot stop this from happening.

Chapter 12

Praise God for His Glory

Moses and the Glory of the LORD

Moses said to the LORD, "You have been telling me, 'Lead these people,' but you have not let me know whom you will send with me. You have said, 'I know you by name and you have found favor with me.' If you are pleased with me, teach me your ways so I may know you and continue to find favor with you. Remember that this nation is your people."

The LORD replied, "My Presence will go with you, and I will give you rest."

Then Moses said to him, "If your Presence does not go with us, do not send us up from here. How will anyone know that you are pleased with me and with your people unless you go with us? What else will distinguish me and your people from all the other people on the face of the earth?"

And the LORD said to Moses, "I will do the very thing you have asked, because I am pleased with you and I know you by name."

Then Moses said, "Now show me your glory."

And the Lord said, "I will cause all my goodness to pass in front of you, and I will proclaim my name, the Lord, in your presence. I will have mercy on whom I will have mercy, and I will have compassion on whom I will have compassion. But," he said, "you cannot see my face, for no one may see me and live."

Then the Lord said, "There is a place near me where you may stand on a rock. When my glory passes by, I will put you in a cleft in the rock and cover you with my hand until I have passed by. Then I will remove my hand and you will see my back; but my face must not be seen." (Exodus 33:12–23 NIV)

God allowed Moses to witness His glory as he passed through, and what a sight Moses must have witnessed from the Lord's back side. Every day we witness the Lord's glory. Numerous have witness miracles from loved ones: lives were spared from tragedy, prayers were answered tremendously every single time, and His forgiving of our sins no man can count. The patience He has with this world is unbelievable.

The Lord is gracious, and full of compassion; slow to anger, and of great mercy.

The Lord is good to all: and his tender mercies are over all his works.

All thy works shall praise thee, O Lord; and thy saints shall bless thee.

They shall speak of the glory of thy kingdom, and talk of thy power. (Psalms 145:8–11)

Chapter 13

Jesus Always Gave God the Glory

Jesus Raises Lazarus from the Dead

Jesus, once more deeply moved, came to the tomb. It was a cave with a stone laid across the entrance. "Take away the stone," he said.

"But, Lord," said Martha, the sister of the dead man, "by this time there is a bad odor, for he has been there four days."

Then Jesus said, "Did I not tell you that if you believe, you will see the glory of God?"

So they took away the stone. Then Jesus looked up and said, "Father, I thank you that you have heard me. I knew that you always hear me, but I said this for the benefit of the people standing here, that they may believe that you sent me."

When he had said this, Jesus called in a loud voice, "Lazarus, come out!" The dead man came out, his hands and feet wrapped with strips of linen, and a cloth around his face.

Jesus said to them, "Take off the grave clothes and let him go."

Jesus stated it well. Then Jesus said, "Did I not tell you that if you believe, you will see the glory of God?" (John 11:38–40 NIV)

We just have to believe what has been spoken in the Word of God, and we will receive. With time and patience, you shall reap a harvest—just do not give up. He is always on time.

Chapter 14

Goodness and Mercy

Again, David gathered together all the chosen men of Israel, thirty thousand.

And David arose, and went with all the people that were with him from Baale of Judah, to bring up from thence the ark of God, whose name is called by the name of the LORD of hosts that dwelleth between the cherubims.

And they set the ark of God upon a new cart, and brought it out of the house of Abinadab that was in Gibeah: and Uzzah and Ahio, the sons of Abinadab, drave the new cart.

And they brought it out of the house of Abinadab which was at Gibeah, accompanying the ark of God: and Ahio went before the ark.

And David and all the house of Israel played before the LORD on all manner of instruments made of fir wood, even on harps, and on psalteries, and on timbrels, and on cornets, and on cymbals. (2 Samuel 6:1–5 King James Bible)

David was a very powerful man who was anointed by God to be king of Israel—although his journey toward his goal was difficult, and it took some time to arrive to victory. All leaders are made to be priest, but not all priests are made to be leaders. God had given

Moses specific instructions how to build the Tabernacle and how to construct the Ark of God. After erecting the Tabernacle, a place where God can dwell among His people, and after building the Ark of God, Moses was no longer allowed to enter the Tabernacle, but God told Him to anoint Aaron his brother, along with Aaron's sons, to be priest. The Ark of God was made from pure gold. No man can have it because they will kill one another just to possess it.

David had the right agenda and the right idea, and he understood what he had (Ark of God). The transportation of it was right, but he did not inform his people about the Ark of God's dos and don'ts.

> And when they came to Nachon's threshingfloor, Uzzah put forth his hand to the ark of God, and took hold of it; for the oxen shook it.
>
> And the anger of the LORD was kindled against Uzzah; and God smote him there for his error; and there he died by the ark of God.
>
> And David was displeased, because the LORD had made a breach upon Uzzah: and he called the name of the place Perezuzzah to this day.
>
> And David was afraid of the LORD that day, and said, How shall the ark of the LORD come to me?
>
> So David would not remove the ark of the LORD unto him into the city of David: but David carried it aside into the house of Obededom the Gittite. (2 Samuel 6:6–10 KJV)

Uzzah did what our instincts tell us to do. It's just like when you throw your child up into air, the child expects you to do what? Catch him! Therefore, Uzzah saw the Ark of God falling and tried to stop its descent by placing his hand on it and lost his life in the process.

The Philistines took the Ark of God from the children of Israel and placed it among their gods, and when they arose the next morning, their gods were down. They repeated the process and came to the conclusion, "We cannot keep the Ark of God among us." It was in the wrong company of people. They placed the Ark of God on two oxen and sent it away. Let me remind you, God led the oxen. The children of Israel were out in the field and saw the Ark of God coming down the road back to where it belonged.

David was afraid to take the Ark of God any further until he had the right understanding how to transport it. The "the house of Obededom" was already chosen by God. It had to be a man who believed in God because the Ark of God cannot be placed just any-where. So while it was there, God started blessing his house. If he had two chickens and a rooster, that was multiplied many times over; now he had more chickens than ever, and every farm animal that he possessed were increased. Each person in the house was blessed tre-mendously. Now if you don't want God in your house, that is your business. Don't get mad because God is in the blessing business. He is going to take care of His children, whether you like or not. This path that God has ordained for me to walk on is hard, but God gets the praise. The Lord not only blesses His children, but He blesses this entire world. We give accordingly, but God gives every day to millions of people, and He blesses the wildlife as well.

God is worthy of praise in more ways than one. After David read the Torah, they came and gave David the report that God was bless-ing the house of Obededom, and it was time for David to retrieve the Ark of God back.

> And it was told king David, saying, The Lord hath blessed the house of Obededom, and all that pertaineth unto him, because of the ark of God. So, David went and brought up the ark of God from the house of Obededom into the city of David with gladness.
>
> And it was so, that when they that bare the ark of the Lord had gone six paces, he sacrificed oxen and fatlings.

And David danced before the LORD with all his might; and David was girded with a linen ephod.

So David and all the house of Israel brought up the ark of the LORD with shouting, and with the sound of the trumpet. (2 Samuel 6:12–15 KJV)

David was a king, but he did mind giving God praise and providing a sacrifice offering to the Lord. David shouted and praised God—"The Lord is my Shepherd and I shall not want!" (Psalm 23). He stripped out of his attire because dancing and shouting heats the body up, but he decided, "We are going to praise Him every six steps and offer sacrifices to His holy name," because God had given them victory.

Chapter 15

Purpose of Praise

That day David first appointed Asaph and his
associates to give praise to the LORD in this
manner:
Give praise to the LORD, proclaim his name;
make known among the nations what he has done.
Sing to him, sing praise to him;
tell of all his wonderful acts.
Glory in his holy name;
let the hearts of those who seek the LORD rejoice.
Look to the LORD and his strength;
seek his face always.
Remember the wonders he has done,
his miracles, and the judgments he pronounced.
(1 Chronicles 16:7–12 NIV)

Why praise Him? The world exists because He exists. Hold on to
your faith and let God lead and guide every step of the way to
your destination. I pray something that you read in this book enters
your heart and soul. Know that "God is still sitting high and earth is
His footstool."

Thank you for reading and listening in Jesus's name. Amen,
amen, amen.

Be blessed.

www.ingramcontent.com/pod-product-compliance
Lightning Source LLC
Chambersburg PA
CBHW021150130726
47988CB00004B/1543